EMMANUEL JOSEPH

The Community Canvas, How Creativity and Compassion Shape Better Decisions and Deeper Bonds

Copyright © 2025 by Emmanuel Joseph

All rights reserved. No part of this publication may be reproduced, stored or transmitted in any form or by any means, electronic, mechanical, photocopying, recording, scanning, or otherwise without written permission from the publisher. It is illegal to copy this book, post it to a website, or distribute it by any other means without permission.

First edition

This book was professionally typeset on Reedsy.
Find out more at reedsy.com

Contents

1	Chapter 1: The Essence of Community	1
2	Chapter 2: The Power of Creative Problem Solving	3
3	Chapter 3: Compassion as a Catalyst for Change	5
4	Chapter 4: The Role of Art in Building Community	7
5	Chapter 5: Empathy in Leadership	9
6	Chapter 6: The Importance of Active Listening	11
7	Chapter 7: Building Inclusive Spaces	13
8	Chapter 8: Fostering Intergenerational Connections	15
9	Chapter 9: The Role of Technology in Community Building	17
10	Chapter 10: The Impact of Volunteering on Community	19
11	Chapter 11: The Role of Education in Community Building	21
12	Chapter 12: The Power of Storytelling in Community Building	23
13	Chapter 13: The Role of Play in Building Community	26
14	Chapter 14: Building Sustainable Communities	28
15	Chapter 15: The Impact of Community Events	30
16	Chapter 16: The Role of Faith and Spirituality in Community...	32
17	Chapter 17: The Future of Community Building	34
18	Chapter 17: The Future of Community Building (continued)	35

1

Chapter 1: The Essence of Community

A community, at its core, is a tapestry woven from the threads of individuals' lives, beliefs, and actions. Each person contributes a unique pattern, adding depth and color to the collective experience. In a world where technology often disconnects us, the essence of community remains a vital force that binds us together. It is through these connections that we find support, encouragement, and a sense of belonging.

Creativity and compassion are the driving forces that shape strong, vibrant communities. When individuals come together with open hearts and minds, they can collaborate on innovative solutions to shared challenges. This synergy fosters a sense of unity and purpose, allowing people to work together toward common goals. In turn, this collective effort strengthens the bonds between community members, creating a resilient and adaptive social fabric.

The importance of community cannot be overstated. It provides a safety net for those in need, offering emotional, financial, and practical support during difficult times. By fostering a culture of empathy and understanding, communities can create an environment where everyone feels valued and included. This sense of belonging is essential for personal growth and well-being, as it encourages individuals to contribute their unique talents and perspectives to the greater good.

In today's fast-paced world, it is more important than ever to nurture and strengthen our communities. By embracing creativity and compassion, we can create a more inclusive, supportive, and resilient society. The following chapters will explore how these qualities can be harnessed to shape better decisions and deeper bonds, ultimately leading to a more connected and thriving world.

2

Chapter 2: The Power of Creative Problem Solving

Creative problem solving is a vital skill that enables individuals and communities to navigate the complexities of modern life. It involves thinking outside the box, challenging conventional wisdom, and finding innovative solutions to pressing issues. By fostering a culture of creativity, communities can adapt to changing circumstances and overcome obstacles more effectively.

One of the key benefits of creative problem solving is its ability to generate multiple solutions to a single problem. This diversity of ideas allows communities to explore various approaches and select the most effective one. Moreover, it encourages collaboration and open dialogue, as individuals share their perspectives and insights. This exchange of ideas can lead to breakthroughs that might not have been possible through conventional methods.

Creativity also plays a crucial role in building resilience within communities. When faced with unexpected challenges, such as natural disasters or economic downturns, creative problem solving enables communities to adapt and recover more quickly. By thinking creatively, individuals can identify new opportunities and resources that can help them overcome adversity. This adaptability is essential for long-term sustainability and growth.

In addition to its practical benefits, creative problem solving fosters a sense of empowerment and agency within communities. When individuals feel that their ideas and contributions are valued, they are more likely to engage actively in community affairs. This increased participation can lead to a more vibrant and dynamic social fabric, where diverse perspectives are respected and celebrated. Ultimately, creative problem solving is a powerful tool that can help communities thrive in an ever-changing world.

3

Chapter 3: Compassion as a Catalyst for Change

Compassion is the cornerstone of a thriving community, as it fosters empathy, understanding, and cooperation among its members. By prioritizing the well-being of others, individuals can create a more inclusive and supportive environment. Compassionate communities are better equipped to address social issues, as they prioritize the needs of the most vulnerable and work together to find solutions.

One of the most significant ways compassion can drive change is by breaking down barriers and fostering inclusivity. When individuals approach others with empathy and understanding, they can bridge cultural, socioeconomic, and generational divides. This inclusivity strengthens the community as a whole, as diverse perspectives and experiences are valued and respected. By embracing compassion, communities can create a more equitable and just society.

Compassion also plays a crucial role in building trust and social cohesion. When individuals feel that their concerns and experiences are acknowledged and validated, they are more likely to engage in open dialogue and collaborate on shared goals. This trust is essential for effective decision-making, as it allows community members to work together towards common objectives. In turn, this collaboration fosters a sense of unity and purpose, strengthening the bonds between individuals.

Moreover, compassion can inspire individuals to take action and make a difference in their communities. By recognizing the struggles and needs of others, individuals can be motivated to contribute their time, resources, and talents to address pressing issues. This collective effort can lead to meaningful and lasting change, as communities work together to create a better future for all. Ultimately, compassion is a powerful catalyst for change, driving communities towards greater harmony and well-being.

4

Chapter 4: The Role of Art in Building Community

Art has the unique ability to bring people together, transcending language and cultural barriers to create a shared experience. It serves as a powerful tool for fostering connections and promoting understanding within communities. By engaging in artistic expression, individuals can explore their emotions, communicate their perspectives, and celebrate their identities. This creative process can lead to a deeper sense of empathy and appreciation for the diverse experiences of others.

Community art projects, such as murals, public installations, and collaborative performances, provide opportunities for individuals to work together towards a common goal. These initiatives can foster a sense of pride and ownership within the community, as members contribute their skills and talents to create something meaningful. Additionally, community art projects can serve as a platform for addressing social issues, sparking conversations, and raising awareness about important topics.

Art also plays a crucial role in preserving and celebrating cultural heritage. By showcasing traditional art forms, communities can honor their history and pass down valuable knowledge to future generations. This cultural preservation fosters a sense of identity and belonging, as individuals connect with their roots and heritage. Moreover, by sharing their cultural traditions with others, communities can promote cross-cultural understanding and appreciation.

Incorporating art into community spaces can also enhance the overall quality of life for residents. Public art installations, community gardens, and cultural events can create vibrant and engaging environments that encourage social interaction and collaboration. These artistic expressions can transform ordinary spaces into places of inspiration and connection, fostering a sense of community and belonging. Ultimately, art is a powerful force that can build bridges, strengthen bonds, and create a more inclusive and compassionate society.

5

Chapter 5: Empathy in Leadership

Empathetic leadership is essential for fostering strong, cohesive communities. Leaders who prioritize empathy are better equipped to understand the needs and concerns of their constituents, allowing them to make more informed and compassionate decisions. By valuing the perspectives and experiences of others, empathetic leaders can create an inclusive environment where everyone feels heard and respected.

One of the key benefits of empathetic leadership is its ability to build trust within the community. When leaders demonstrate genuine concern for the well-being of their constituents, they inspire confidence and loyalty. This trust is crucial for effective decision-making, as it encourages open dialogue and collaboration. By fostering a culture of empathy, leaders can create a supportive and cooperative community that is better equipped to address shared challenges.

Empathetic leaders also play a vital role in promoting social justice and equity. By recognizing and addressing systemic inequalities, they can create a more inclusive and fair society. This commitment to social justice is essential for fostering a sense of belonging and empowerment within the community. When individuals feel that their voices are valued and their needs are prioritized, they are more likely to engage actively in community affairs.

Moreover, empathetic leadership can inspire others to adopt a more compassionate approach in their interactions. By leading by example, empathetic leaders can create a ripple effect, encouraging others to prioritize empathy and understanding in their own lives. This collective commitment to empathy can strengthen the social fabric of the community, fostering deeper connections and a greater sense of unity. Ultimately, empathy in leadership is a powerful force that can drive positive change and create a more harmonious and resilient community.

6

Chapter 6: The Importance of Active Listening

Active listening is a crucial skill that fosters understanding, empathy, and connection within communities. By fully engaging with others and validating their experiences, individuals can create a supportive and inclusive environment. Active listening involves not only hearing the words being spoken but also understanding the emotions and intentions behind them. This deeper level of engagement can lead to more meaningful and productive conversations.

One of the key benefits of active listening is its ability to build trust and rapport between individuals. When people feel that their concerns and experiences are genuinely acknowledged, they are more likely to open up and share their thoughts. This openness fosters a sense of connection and mutual respect, strengthening the bonds within the community. By prioritizing active listening, individuals can create a more inclusive and supportive social fabric.

Active listening also plays a vital role in effective problem-solving and decision-making. By understanding the diverse perspectives and needs of community members, individuals can develop more informed and compassionate solutions. This collaborative approach encourages open dialogue and ensures that everyone's voice is heard. In turn, this can lead to more innovative and effective outcomes that address the needs of the entire community.

Moreover, active listening can help to resolve conflicts and misunderstandings within the community. By approaching disagreements with empathy and understanding, individuals can identify the root causes of the issue and work together to find a resolution. This collaborative approach can prevent escalation and foster a sense of unity and cooperation. Ultimately, active listening is a powerful tool that can strengthen relationships, promote understanding, and create a more connected and resilient community.

7

Chapter 7: Building Inclusive Spaces

Creating inclusive spaces is ensuring accessibility for all individuals. This involves addressing physical, social, and cultural barriers that may prevent people from fully participating in community activities. By creating environments that are accessible to everyone, communities can ensure that all members have the opportunity to engage and contribute.

Another important aspect of building inclusive spaces is fostering a culture of respect and understanding. This involves actively challenging stereotypes, prejudices, and discrimination that may exist within the community. By promoting open dialogue and encouraging individuals to share their experiences, communities can create a more inclusive and supportive environment. This cultural shift can help to break down barriers and build trust among community members.

Inclusive spaces also provide opportunities for individuals to learn from one another and grow. By bringing together people from diverse backgrounds, communities can create rich and dynamic environments where individuals can share their knowledge, skills, and perspectives. This exchange of ideas can lead to new insights and innovations, fostering a sense of collective growth and development.

Ultimately, building inclusive spaces is about creating environments where everyone feels valued and respected. By prioritizing accessibility, respect, and understanding, communities can create a more inclusive and supportive social fabric. This inclusivity can lead to stronger connections and deeper bonds among community members, fostering a sense of unity and belonging.

8

Chapter 8: Fostering Intergenerational Connections

Intergenerational connections are essential for building strong, cohesive communities. By fostering relationships between individuals of different ages, communities can create a more inclusive and supportive environment. These connections provide opportunities for learning, mentorship, and mutual support, fostering a sense of unity and belonging.

One of the key benefits of intergenerational connections is the exchange of knowledge and skills. Older individuals can share their wisdom and experience with younger generations, while younger individuals can offer fresh perspectives and new ideas. This exchange can lead to a deeper understanding and appreciation of different life stages, fostering a sense of respect and empathy.

Intergenerational connections also provide opportunities for mentorship and support. Older individuals can serve as role models and mentors for younger generations, offering guidance and encouragement. This mentorship can help to build confidence and resilience in younger individuals, fostering their personal and professional growth. In turn, younger individuals can offer support and assistance to older community members, creating a sense of reciprocity and mutual care.

Moreover, intergenerational connections can help to bridge generational divides and foster social cohesion. By encouraging individuals of different ages to engage with one another, communities can break down stereotypes and misconceptions that may exist between generations. This can lead to a more inclusive and understanding social fabric, where individuals of all ages feel valued and respected.

Ultimately, fostering intergenerational connections is essential for building strong, resilient communities. By creating opportunities for individuals of different ages to connect and learn from one another, communities can create a more inclusive and supportive environment. This can lead to deeper bonds and a greater sense of unity and belonging among community members.

9

Chapter 9: The Role of Technology in Community Building

Technology has the potential to revolutionize the way communities connect and collaborate. By leveraging digital tools and platforms, communities can enhance communication, streamline decision-making, and foster a sense of belonging. However, it is essential to use technology mindfully and inclusively to ensure that all community members can benefit from its advantages.

One of the key benefits of technology in community building is its ability to facilitate communication and information sharing. Digital platforms, such as social media, messaging apps, and online forums, provide opportunities for individuals to connect and engage with one another. This can help to break down geographical barriers and create a sense of community among individuals who may not have the opportunity to interact in person.

Technology can also streamline decision-making and collaboration within communities. Digital tools, such as project management software and collaborative platforms, can facilitate the sharing of ideas and resources. This can lead to more efficient and effective problem-solving, as community members can work together towards common goals. Additionally, technology can provide opportunities for community members to participate in decision-making processes, fostering a sense of ownership and accountability.

However, it is essential to use technology mindfully and inclusively. Not all community members may have access to digital tools or the skills to use them effectively. By prioritizing digital literacy and accessibility, communities can ensure that all members can benefit from the advantages of technology. This may involve providing training and support for individuals who may be less familiar with digital tools, as well as addressing barriers to access, such as cost and connectivity.

Ultimately, technology has the potential to enhance community building and foster deeper connections among members. By using digital tools mindfully and inclusively, communities can create a more connected and resilient social fabric. This can lead to stronger bonds and a greater sense of unity and belonging among community members.

10

Chapter 10: The Impact of Volunteering on Community

Volunteering is a powerful way for individuals to contribute to their communities and make a positive impact. By offering their time, skills, and resources, volunteers can address pressing social issues and support those in need. Volunteering also provides opportunities for personal growth and connection, fostering a sense of purpose and belonging.

One of the key benefits of volunteering is its ability to address community needs and challenges. Volunteers can provide essential services and support for vulnerable individuals, such as food distribution, healthcare, and education. This collective effort can help to alleviate social issues and create a more equitable and just society. By working together, volunteers can make a significant difference in the lives of others and contribute to the overall well-being of the community.

Volunteering also provides opportunities for personal growth and development. By engaging in volunteer activities, individuals can develop new skills, gain valuable experience, and build confidence. This can lead to greater self-awareness and a sense of accomplishment, fostering personal growth and well-being. Additionally, volunteering can provide opportunities for individuals to explore their interests and passions, leading to a more fulfilling and purposeful life.

Moreover, volunteering can foster a sense of connection and belonging within the community. By working together towards common goals, volunteers can build relationships and create a sense of camaraderie. This social connection can lead to deeper bonds and a greater sense of unity among community members. Additionally, volunteering can provide opportunities for individuals to meet new people and expand their social networks, fostering a more inclusive and supportive social fabric.

Ultimately, volunteering is a powerful way for individuals to contribute to their communities and make a positive impact. By offering their time, skills, and resources, volunteers can address pressing social issues and support those in need. This collective effort can lead to stronger bonds and a greater sense of unity and belonging among community members.

11

Chapter 11: The Role of Education in Community Building

Education plays a crucial role in building strong, cohesive communities. By providing individuals with the knowledge, skills, and values they need to thrive, education can foster personal growth and social development. Additionally, education can promote social cohesion and inclusivity by creating opportunities for individuals to learn from one another and develop a shared understanding of the world.

One of the key benefits of education is its ability to empower individuals and promote personal growth. By providing access to knowledge and skills, education can help individuals reach their full potential and achieve their goals. This empowerment can lead to greater self-confidence and a sense of agency, fostering personal growth and well-being. Additionally, education can provide individuals with the tools they need to navigate the complexities of modern life and contribute to the overall well-being of the community.

Education also plays a vital role in promoting social cohesion and inclusivity. By bringing together individuals from diverse backgrounds, educational institutions can create opportunities for cross-cultural understanding and collaboration. This exchange of ideas and perspectives can lead to a deeper appreciation for diversity and a greater sense of unity among community members. Additionally, education can promote social justice and equity by addressing systemic inequalities and providing opportunities for all individuals to succeed.

Moreover, education can foster a sense of community and belonging within educational institutions. By creating supportive and inclusive learning environments, educators can help students build strong relationships and develop a sense of connection. This sense of belonging can lead to greater engagement and participation in community affairs, fostering a more vibrant and dynamic social fabric.

Ultimately, education is essential for building strong, cohesive communities. By providing individuals with the knowledge, skills, and values they need to thrive, education can promote personal growth, social cohesion, and inclusivity. This can lead to deeper bonds and a greater sense of unity and belonging among community members.

12

Chapter 12: The Power of Storytelling in Community Building

Storytelling is a powerful tool for building connections and fostering understanding within communities. By sharing their experiences and perspectives, individuals can create a sense of empathy and appreciation for the diverse experiences of others. Storytelling can also preserve cultural heritage and promote a sense of identity and belonging, fostering a more inclusive and cohesive social fabric.

One of the key benefits of storytelling is its ability to create a sense of empathy and understanding. By sharing their personal experiences, individuals can help others see the world from their perspective and appreciate the challenges and triumphs they have faced. This empathy can lead to a deeper sense of connection and mutual respect, strengthening the bonds within the community.

Storytelling also plays a crucial role in preserving and celebrating cultural heritage. By sharing traditional stories, myths, and legends, communities can honor their history and pass down valuable knowledge to future generations. This cultural preservation fosters a sense of identity and belonging, as individuals connect with their roots and heritage. Moreover, by sharing their cultural traditions with others, communities can promote cross-cultural understanding and appreciation.

In addition to its cultural benefits, storytelling can also promote social change and advocacy. By sharing their stories, individuals can raise awareness about important social issues and inspire others to take action. This can lead to greater engagement and participation in community affairs, fostering a more just and equitable society. Storytelling can also provide a platform for marginalized voices, giving them the opportunity to share their experiences and advocate for their rights.

Ultimately, Storytelling is a powerful tool for building connections and fostering understanding within communities. By sharing their experiences and perspectives, individuals can create a sense of empathy and appreciation for the diverse experiences of others. Storytelling can also preserve cultural heritage and promote a sense of identity and belonging, fostering a more inclusive and cohesive social fabric.

One of the key benefits of storytelling is its ability to create a sense of empathy and understanding. By sharing their personal experiences, individuals can help others see the world from their perspective and appreciate the challenges and triumphs they have faced. This empathy can lead to a deeper sense of connection and mutual respect, strengthening the bonds within the community.

Storytelling also plays a crucial role in preserving and celebrating cultural heritage. By sharing traditional stories, myths, and legends, communities can honor their history and pass down valuable knowledge to future generations. This cultural preservation fosters a sense of identity and belonging, as individuals connect with their roots and heritage. Moreover, by sharing their cultural traditions with others, communities can promote cross-cultural understanding and appreciation.

In addition to its cultural benefits, storytelling can also promote social change and advocacy. By sharing their stories, individuals can raise awareness about important social issues and inspire others to take action. This can lead to greater engagement and participation in community affairs, fostering a more just and equitable society. Storytelling can also provide a platform for marginalized voices, giving them the opportunity to share their experiences and advocate for their rights.

Ultimately, storytelling is a powerful tool for building connections and fostering understanding within communities. By sharing their experiences and perspectives, individuals can create a sense of empathy and appreciation for the diverse experiences of others. Storytelling can also preserve cultural heritage and promote a sense of identity and belonging, fostering a more inclusive and cohesive social fabric.

13

Chapter 13: The Role of Play in Building Community

Play is an essential element of human experience that fosters creativity, connection, and well-being. By engaging in playful activities, individuals can build relationships, reduce stress, and explore new ideas. Incorporating play into community life can create a more vibrant and dynamic social fabric, fostering a sense of unity and belonging.

One of the key benefits of play is its ability to build relationships and strengthen social bonds. Playful activities, such as sports, games, and creative projects, provide opportunities for individuals to connect and collaborate. This shared experience can lead to a deeper sense of trust and camaraderie, fostering a sense of unity within the community. By prioritizing play, communities can create a more inclusive and supportive environment where everyone feels valued and connected.

Play also plays a crucial role in promoting mental and emotional well-being. Engaging in playful activities can reduce stress, boost mood, and enhance cognitive function. This can lead to greater resilience and overall well-being, enabling individuals to navigate the challenges of modern life more effectively. By incorporating play into community life, communities can create a more supportive and nurturing environment that promotes the well-being of all members.

CHAPTER 13: THE ROLE OF PLAY IN BUILDING COMMUNITY

Moreover, play fosters creativity and innovation. Playful activities encourage individuals to think outside the box, explore new ideas, and take risks. This creative process can lead to new insights and breakthroughs, fostering a sense of growth and development within the community. By embracing play, communities can create a more dynamic and innovative social fabric that is better equipped to address shared challenges and opportunities.

Ultimately, play is an essential element of community building that fosters creativity, connection, and well-being. By incorporating play into community life, communities can create a more vibrant and dynamic social fabric, fostering a sense of unity and belonging. This can lead to stronger bonds and a greater sense of unity and belonging among community members.

14

Chapter 14: Building Sustainable Communities

Sustainability is a vital consideration for building strong, resilient communities. By prioritizing environmental, social, and economic sustainability, communities can create a more equitable and just society that meets the needs of current and future generations. Sustainable communities are better equipped to adapt to changing circumstances and address shared challenges, fostering a sense of unity and resilience.

One of the key elements of building sustainable communities is promoting environmental stewardship. By prioritizing conservation, renewable energy, and sustainable practices, communities can reduce their environmental impact and protect natural resources for future generations. This commitment to environmental sustainability fosters a sense of responsibility and care for the planet, creating a more harmonious and resilient social fabric.

Social sustainability is also essential for building strong, cohesive communities. This involves addressing social issues, such as poverty, inequality, and discrimination, and promoting inclusivity and social justice. By prioritizing social sustainability, communities can create a more equitable and just society where everyone feels valued and supported. This inclusivity fosters a sense of unity and belonging, strengthening the bonds within the community.

Economic sustainability is another crucial element of building sustainable communities. This involves creating economic opportunities and stability for all community members, promoting fair wages, and supporting local businesses. By prioritizing economic sustainability, communities can create a more resilient and vibrant economy that benefits everyone. This economic stability fosters a sense of security and well-being, enabling individuals to thrive and contribute to the overall well-being of the community.

Ultimately, building sustainable communities is essential for creating a more equitable, just, and resilient society. By prioritizing environmental, social, and economic sustainability, communities can create a more inclusive and supportive environment that meets the needs of current and future generations. This sustainability fosters a sense of unity and resilience, enabling communities to adapt and thrive in an ever-changing world.

15

Chapter 15: The Impact of Community Events

Community events are powerful tools for fostering connection, celebration, and engagement within communities. By bringing people together, community events create opportunities for individuals to connect, share their experiences, and celebrate their shared identity. These events can strengthen the social fabric of the community, fostering a sense of unity and belonging.

One of the key benefits of community events is their ability to create a sense of celebration and joy. Events such as festivals, parades, and cultural celebrations provide opportunities for individuals to come together and celebrate their shared identity and heritage. This sense of celebration fosters a sense of pride and belonging, strengthening the bonds within the community. By prioritizing community events, communities can create a more vibrant and dynamic social fabric.

Community events also provide opportunities for engagement and participation. By involving community members in the planning and execution of events, communities can create a sense of ownership and accountability. This engagement fosters a sense of unity and cooperation, as individuals work together towards common goals. Additionally, community events can provide opportunities for individuals to share their talents, skills, and perspectives,

CHAPTER 15: THE IMPACT OF COMMUNITY EVENTS

fostering a sense of appreciation and respect.

Moreover, community events can address social issues and promote social change. Events such as awareness campaigns, charity drives, and community forums provide opportunities for individuals to learn about important social issues and take action. This engagement can lead to greater awareness and participation in community affairs, fostering a more just and equitable society.

Ultimately, community events are powerful tools for fostering connection, celebration, and engagement within communities. By bringing people together, community events create opportunities for individuals to connect, share their experiences, and celebrate their shared identity. These events can strengthen the social fabric of the community, fostering a sense of unity and belonging.

16

Chapter 16: The Role of Faith and Spirituality in Community Building

Faith and spirituality play a crucial role in building strong, cohesive communities. By providing individuals with a sense of purpose, belonging, and connection, faith and spirituality can foster a sense of unity and resilience. Communities that prioritize faith and spirituality create supportive and inclusive environments where individuals can thrive.

One of the key benefits of faith and spirituality is their ability to provide individuals with a sense of purpose and meaning. By offering a framework for understanding the world and one's place in it, faith and spirituality can foster a sense of direction and fulfillment. This sense of purpose can lead to greater resilience and well-being, enabling individuals to navigate the challenges of modern life more effectively.

Faith and spirituality also play a vital role in fostering a sense of connection and belonging. By bringing individuals together in worship, prayer, and community activities, faith communities create opportunities for individuals to build relationships and strengthen social bonds. This sense of belonging fosters a sense of unity and cooperation, as individuals support and care for one another.

Moreover, faith and spirituality can inspire individuals to take action and make a positive impact in their communities. By promoting values such as compassion, justice, and service, faith communities can motivate individuals to contribute their time, resources, and talents to address pressing social issues. This collective effort can lead to meaningful and lasting change, fostering a more just and equitable society.

Ultimately, faith and spirituality play a crucial role in building strong, cohesive communities. By providing individuals with a sense of purpose, belonging, and connection, faith and spirituality can foster a sense of unity and resilience. Communities that prioritize faith and spirituality create supportive and inclusive environments where individuals can thrive.

17

Chapter 17: The Future of Community Building

As we look to the future, it is essential to consider how we can continue to build strong, resilient communities. By prioritizing creativity, compassion, and collaboration, communities can adapt to changing circumstances and address shared challenges. The future of community building lies in our ability to innovate, connect, and support one another.

One of the key elements of the future of community building is harnessing the power of technology. Digital tools and platforms have the potential to revolutionize the way communities connect and collaborate. By leveraging technology mindfully and inclusively, communities can enhance communication, streamline decision-making, and foster a sense of belonging. This can lead to stronger bonds and a greater sense of unity among community members.

Another important aspect of the future of community building is promoting sustainability. By prioritizing environmental, social, and economic sustainability, communities can create a more equitable and just society that meets the needs of current and future generations. This sustainability fosters a sense of unity and resilience, enabling communities to adapt and thrive in an ever-changing world.

18

Chapter 17: The Future of Community Building (continued)

Moreover, the future of community building lies in fostering collaboration and mutual support. By working together towards common goals, communities can create a more inclusive and supportive environment. This collective effort can lead to meaningful and lasting change, fostering a sense of unity and belonging among community members. By prioritizing creativity, compassion, and collaboration, we can build stronger, more resilient communities that are better equipped to navigate the challenges of the future.

In conclusion, the future of community building is bright, as long as we continue to harness the power of creativity and compassion. By embracing these qualities and working together, we can create a more connected and thriving world. The following chapters will explore how these qualities can be harnessed to shape better decisions and deeper bonds, ultimately leading to a more connected and thriving world.

Book Description

"The Community Canvas: How Creativity and Compassion Shape Better Decisions and Deeper Bonds" is an inspiring exploration of the power of community. This thought-provoking book delves into the essential elements that make communities strong, resilient, and connected. Through

17 engaging chapters, the book highlights the importance of creativity, compassion, and collaboration in building vibrant communities that can adapt to changing circumstances and address shared challenges.

From the essence of community and the power of creative problem-solving to the role of faith and spirituality, each chapter offers valuable insights and practical strategies for fostering connection and inclusivity. The book also explores the impact of art, play, and storytelling in building community, as well as the importance of education, volunteering, and active listening. Additionally, the book examines the role of technology and sustainability in creating a more equitable and just society.

"The Community Canvas" is a must-read for anyone passionate about building stronger, more resilient communities. With its compelling stories, practical advice, and inspiring vision for the future, this book is a valuable resource for community leaders, educators, activists, and anyone looking to make a positive impact in their community.

www.ingramcontent.com/pod-product-compliance
Lightning Source LLC
LaVergne TN
LVHW020457080526
838202LV00057B/5999